The Delightful sales success

Achieving profitable result through Delighting sales techniques

By

Donovan Alston

Copyright © **2023**

No part of this book may be reproduced or transmitted in any form or by any means, including
Photocopy, recording or other electronic or mechanical method without the prior written permission of the publisher, except in the case of brief quotation embodied in review and certain other noncommercial uses permitted by copyright laws

Table of content

Introduction

In today's highly competitive and ever-evolving business environment, achieving sales success is more than just a goal; it is a journey. Welcome to "The Great Deals Achievement," where we embark on an enamoring investigation of the methodologies, strategies, and rules that lead to standard deal accomplishments yet exceptional and brilliant ones. In the following pages, we'll show you how to create memorable sales experiences, cultivate long-term customer relationships, and ultimately turn satisfied customers into devoted advocates. In the world of sales, success is frequently measured by revenue generated and targets achieved. Come along with us as we navigate the delightful landscape of sales success, where every interaction becomes an opportunity and every sale is a celebration of accomplishments. However, what distinguishes truly remarkable sales success from ordinary success? It's the joy factor—exceeding all expectations to create an uncommon encounter for the two clients and deal experts. Delightful Sales Success" is the term we use to describe this.

Success in sales is more than just getting deals closed and meeting quotas; it's about building real relationships with customers and making sure they're happy throughout the entire process. It requires comprehending their requirements, tailoring solutions, and exceeding their expectations. In addition to increasing sales, this strategy builds long-term customer advocacy and loyalty.

Besides, the idea of awesome deal achievement reaches past client corporations. It likewise stresses the prosperity and satisfaction of the deal experts themselves. Sales teams can consistently produce outstanding results and enjoy their work when they are empowered, supported, and motivated. A healthy climate cultivates development, supports imagination, and celebrates accomplishments.

Chapter 1:

The force of building client relationships

In the present profoundly aggressive business scene, achievement is not set in stone by the nature of your item or administration. It depends equally, if not more, on your capacity to build lasting relationships with customers. This part investigates the significant effect that building client connections can have on your business.

Why client connections matter

Relationships with customers are essential to any successful business. Building a meaningful relationship with your customers can help you achieve more than just a sale.

Customer Retention

At the point when clients feel a veritable association with your image, they are bound to stay steadfast, picking your items or administrations over contenders.

Peer-to-Peer Marketing:

Your brand ambassadors spread positive word-of-mouth and attract new customers from satisfied clients.

Repeat Activity:

Strong relationships encourage repeat business, which boosts profitability and revenue.

Reviews and enhancements:

You'll be able to stay competitive thanks to the valuable customer feedback you receive from close relationships.

Building Relationships with Customers "Personalization:

Tailor your communications with clients to their singular inclinations and necessities. Personalization can be as straightforward as addressing them by name in emails or as complicated as making product recommendations that are specific to them.

Compelling Correspondence:

Utilize a variety of channels to communicate with customers on a regular basis, including email, social media, and even in-person meetings. Keep them informed about updates, advancements, and new contributions.

Listening:

Actively pay attention to feedback from customers, whether it's praise or criticism. Make the necessary adjustments based on this feedback and demonstrate to customers that their opinions are important.

Excellent customer care:

To provide exceptional customer service, go above and beyond. Take care of issues immediately and make the client's insight as smooth as could be expected.

Promoting Trust:

Trust is the foundation of any solid relationship. In your interactions with customers, be transparent, sincere, and trustworthy.

Estimating Achievement

Building client connections is certainly not a theoretical idea; it's a quantifiable and vital exertion. Consider utilizing key execution markers, for example, client standards for dependability, Net Advertiser Score, and consumer loyalty overviews, to measure the adequacy of your relationship-building efforts.

Case Analysis:

Fruitful relationship building To represent the force of building client connections, we'll dive into a contextual analysis of an organization that has succeeded from this viewpoint. We'll talk about their strategies, the difficulties they faced, and the outcomes they got from their customer-centric approach. From utilizing technology to mastering the art of customer feedback, we will delve deeper into specific methods and strategies for successful relationship building in the following chapters. By the end of this book, you will know everything there is to know about how building strong relationships with customers can be the driving force behind your business's success.

Understanding the significance of laying out serious areas of strength

associations with clients

In the dynamic and consistently developing universe of business, one truth remains: Your success is based on your customers. Laying out areas of strength for your clients isn't simply a choice; it is a fundamental part of any flourishing endeavor. This chapter explains why developing these connections is crucial to the success and longevity of your business.

The client-driven worldview

Present-day business has moved from an item-driven approach to a client-driven one. In this new worldview, clients are purchasers as well as accomplices in your prosperity process. Here's the reason understanding the significance of laying out areas of strength with clients is vital:

Unwaveringly and Maintenance:

Customers are more likely to stick with your company if they feel appreciated and connected to it. Steadfast clients contribute essentially to your income through recurrent business. Social media marketing: fulfilled clients become energetic backers for your image. They share their positive encounters with others, successfully promoting your business at no expense to you.

Input and Improvement:

Connections with customers are a great way to get feedback. Honest feedback from customers enables you to identify innovation and improvement opportunities.

Resilience in the face of competition

A strong customer base can prevent competitors from entering competitive markets. A trusted brand often attracts higher prices from customers.

The human element in business

In an era when technology plays a significant role in customer interactions, the significance of the human touch is easy to overlook. Personal connections, however, continue to be essential. Individuals believe they should work with others, not anonymous enterprises. This is the way you can bridle the human component in building associations: Empathy: Know what your customers want, need, and worry about. Show real compassion in your collaborations, exhibiting that you care about their prosperity.

Strategies for fostering long-term relationships

An overview of the chapter titled "Strategies for Fostering Long-Term Relationships" is provided below. Strategies for Fostering Long-Term Relationships Introduction: In both personal and professional lives, it is essential to establish and maintain long-term relationships. This chapter looks at effective ways to nurture and keep these important connections going. The key is communication. Viable correspondence lies at the core of any fruitful long-haul relationship. Transparent exchange, undivided attention, and sympathy are essential parts that assist with building trust and understanding between people.

Fidelity and Openness:

Trust is the foundation of enduring connections. Being straightforward, solid, and steady in your activities encourages trust. Staying away from trickery and maintaining respectability are basic to maintaining this trust over the long run

Resolution of Conflict:

Struggle is unavoidable in any relationship. Figuring out how to address clashes helpfully, as opposed to staying away from or heightening them, is significant. Methods like dynamic critical thinking and compromise can assist with settling issues without causing lasting harm. Emotional Capacity: Understanding one's own emotions as well as those of others is an essential part of emotional intelligence. This expertise supports dealing with feelings, communicating sympathy, and interfacing on a more profound level with individuals, which is fundamental for long-haul securities.

Common Objectives and Values:

Enduring connections frequently flourish when people share normal qualities, interests, and objectives. By providing a sense of purpose and direction, finding common ground can assist in maintaining the connection.

Time and Exertion:

Putting time and exertion into connections is an unquestionable requirement. Routinely checking in, getting to know each other, and showing appreciation for each other's commitments are straightforward yet strong ways of sustaining associations.

Adaptability:

Relationships need to adjust to the ever-changing nature of life. Being adaptable and able to conform to developing conditions guarantees that connections stay versatile and keep on developing.

Boundaries:

Defining and regarding limits is fundamental for keeping up with solid connections. People should be willing to respect others' boundaries and clearly communicate their needs and boundaries.

Appreciation and Acknowledgement:

Relationships can be strengthened by expressing gratitude and recognizing the value of others. Little tokens of appreciation go a long way toward encouraging altruism and unwavering loyalty.

Forgiveness:

Forgiveness is an essential component of any enduring relationship because mistakes do occur. Figuring out how to pardon and push ahead instead of harping on past complaints is fundamental for development and life span.

Conclusion:The methodologies framed in this part give a guide to supporting long-haul connections. Whether in private or expert settings, these standards provide people with areas of strength for building associations that can advance their daily routines and the existence of those around them.

Building trust and dependability through brilliant client assistance

In the present cutthroat business scene, building trust and reliability with clients is fundamental to long-term achievement. This chapter delves into the art and science of providing exceptional customer service that not only satisfies customers but also transforms them into devoted advocates of your brand.

Figuring out client assumptions

Investigate how client assumptions have advanced in the computerized age and the role they play in forming client care systems. To build trust, talk about how important it is to match your company's goals with what customers want.

The Force of Consistency

Feature the meaning of consistency in conveying first-rate client assistance. Give concrete examples of businesses that have done a great job of maintaining consistent service quality.

Correspondence

Accentuate the job of clear and sympathetic correspondence in settling client issues and encouraging trust. Give tips and strategies for further developing relational abilities among client assistance groups.Compelling

Personalization and Customization

Make sense of how personalization and customization can improve the client experience. Provide insight into how to tailor services to individual preferences by utilizing data and technology. Taking care of client complaints: share best practices for dealing with client grievances with beauty and transforming them into open doors for building trust. Provide a step-by-step guide for developing efficient procedures for resolving complaints.

Customer service teams emphasize the

significance of investing in employee empowerment and training. Talk about procedures for propelling and preparing client care agents to succeed in their jobs.

Measuring Satisfaction among Customers

Implement key performance indicators for evaluating customer satisfaction. Explain how to continuously improve service quality by gathering and analyzing customer feedback.

Making a client-driven culture

Depict how to impart a client-driven outlook all through the association. Showcase businesses whose cultures have successfully changed to put customers first.

Faithfulness Projects and Maintenance Procedures

Investigate the role of faithfulness programs in holding clients. Give instances of viable dependability methodologies and their effect on long-haul client relationships. in

Building confidence in the advanced age

Talk about the novel difficulties and chances of building trust in an undeniably computerized world. To earn the trust of online customers, offer strategies for ensuring transparency and safety. Contextual analyses of client support excellence Analyze contextual analyses from different enterprises, featuring organizations that have succeeded in

Chapter 2

Dominating Successful correspondence in deals

Presentation: In the realm of deals, correspondence is the bedrock upon which fruitful exchanges are constructed. Whether you're selling items, services, or thoughts, your capacity to really speak with likely clients can be the deciding moment in an arrangement. This section will dig into the fundamental parts of dominating compelling correspondence in deals, offering reasonable tips, systems, and bits of knowledge to assist you in turning into an additional enticing and persuasive deal proficient.

Segment 1:

The Art of Active Listening Active listening is the first step toward effective communication. You must truly comprehend your prospects' wants, needs, and challenges in order to connect with them. In this segment, we will investigate the significance of listening intently in sales. Methods for improving your undivided attention abilities How to ask questions that are open-ended and lead to valuable information methods for demonstrating empathy and establishing rapport

Segment 2:

Customizing Your Message In sales, one-size-fits-all communication fails. To find true success, you should tailor your message to each prospect's exceptional inclinations and requirements. This section will discuss the idea of client personas and why they matter. adjusting your communication style to reflect the personality of your prospect. developing convincing value propositions. engaging and persuading through storytelling.

Segment 3:

Conquering complaints and building trust Discussions frequently include protests and distrust. It is essential to master the skill of overcoming objections and establishing trust. In this section, we'll talk about: Normal protests and how to really address them Methodologies for building trust and validity The job of social verification and tributes in correspondence is to handle objections with grace to maintain a positive flow of conversation.

Segment 4

The ultimate objective of effective sales communication is to close a sale. This segment will explore different shutting strategies and when to utilize them.

recognizing and responding to buying cues. Instructions to make a need to keep moving without pressure.

strategies for following up to close the deal.

Conclusion: Dominating powerful correspondence in deals is a continuous cycle that requires commitment and practice. You can significantly improve your sales success by actively listening, tailoring your message, overcoming objections, and skillfully closing deals. In this part, we've given significant bits of knowledge and systems to assist you with exploring the mind-boggling universe of deal correspondence, eventually prompting expanded transformations and fulfilled clients.

Increasing one's ability to communicate effectively in order to engage and persuade customers Introduction:

In the present serious business scene, powerful relational abilities are vital for drawing in and convincing clients. Whether you're a salesperson, a marketer, or the owner of a business, mastering the art of communication can mean the difference between making a sale and missing out on opportunities. This section will investigate key systems and procedures to create and level up your correspondence abilities to really dazzle and persuade your clients.

Segment 1:

Understanding client brain research To draw in and convince clients, it's fundamental to comprehend the brain science behind their dynamic cycles. Consumer behavior, emotional triggers, and cognitive biases that influence customer choices will all be examined in this section. You'll be better able to tailor your communication to their needs and desires if you understand these fundamental concepts.

Segment 2:

Empathy and active listening are two of the most important aspects of effective communication. Learn how to truly connect with your customers by focusing on their concerns, requirements, and preferences. Develop a stronger foundation for persuasion by learning strategies for empathizing with others and establishing rapport.

Segment 3:

Making persuasive messages In this section, you will learn how to make messages that appeal to your intended audience. Explore the power of storytelling, how to structure your messages to make the most of their impact, and how to back up your claims with data and evidence. You can effectively communicate your value proposition if you master these skills.

Segmen 4

Nonverbal Communication Communication involves more than just speaking; nonverbal signals play a critical role. To make your message more persuasive, learn how to use body language, facial expressions, and gestures effectively. Find ways to adjust your nonverbal correspondence to your verbal substance for a really convincing show.

Segment 5

Overcoming Objections In every interaction with a customer, there will be objections or concerns. This part will give methodologies for dealing with complaints effortlessly, tending to client questions, and transforming them into open doors for influence. You'll acquire procedures to expect protests and prepare for successful reactions.

Segment 6:

Establishing credibility and trusting relationships with customers is built on trust. Investigate strategies for establishing and maintaining credibility and trust with your clients. Grasp the job of straightforwardness, consistency, and moral correspondence in laying out long-haul truss

Segment 7:

Adjusting to Different Correspondence Diverts In the present computerized age, correspondence happens through different channels, including email, online entertainment, and in-person gatherings. Learn to adapt your communication skills to various platforms to guarantee consistency and efficacy across channels.

Segment 8:

Contextual investigations and down-to-earth activities This part will conclude with genuine contextual analyses and pragmatic activities. You will be able to put the communication techniques and skills learned in the chapter into practice through these examples and activities, which will help you improve your skills even further. Conclusion: An ongoing process that can have a significant impact on your company's success is learning how to communicate effectively in order to engage and persuade customers. You will be well-prepared to succeed in the modern market by mastering the psychological aspects of customer behavior, active listening, crafting compelling messages, nonverbal communication, handling objections, establishing trust, and adapting to various channels. A comprehensive guide to improving your communication skills and ultimately improving customer engagement and persuasion is provided in this chapter.

The Craft of Undivided Attention to Comprehend Client Needs and

Inclinations

In the present exceptionally aggressive business scene, understanding client needs and inclinations is pivotal for the outcome of any association. Companies that do well in this area often know how to listen actively. The significance of active listening in comprehending customer needs and preferences will also be discussed in this chapter.

as well as offer helpful methods for improving this ability

1

Enhancing Customer Engagement: The Importance of Active Listening

Undivided attention is urgent when identifying areas of strength for clients. By effectively paying attention to their interests, feelings, and wants, organizations can actually draw in their clients, building trust and dedication.

Uncovering Neglected Client Needs

An organization can identify unmet needs and preferences that customers may not readily express through active listening. Businesses can gain a competitive advantage by customizing their products or services to better meet customer needs by collecting this valuable data.

2:

Key Components of Undivided Attention

Mindfulness: Maintain eye contact, pay full attention to the speaker, and demonstrate your interest in the conversation. Nonverbal Correspondence: To demonstrate your interest and comprehension, make use of appropriate body language, such as facial expressions or nodding. Empathy: Make an effort to comprehend the speaker's feelings and point of view. Empathize with them by acknowledging their feelings. Prevent disruption: Try not to hinder or complete the speaker's sentences. Before responding, allow them to fully express themselves. Intelligent Reactions: Give the speaker feedback to show that you understand. To ensure that you have understood what they have said, repeat it or rephrase it. Questions that could go either way: Encourage the speaker to elaborate and share more by asking questions that are open-ended. Insignificant Encouragers: Utilize short expressions like "I see," "Go on," or "Let me know more" to urge the speaker to proceed. Summarization: Recap what you've heard on a regular basis to show that you're paying attention and that you have understood. Stay away from judgment. Avoid judging others or offering immediate solutions. Your job is to tune in, not scrutinize or tackle issues immediately. Respect: Recognize the speaker's considerations, conclusions, and encounters, regardless of whether you disagree. Rehearsing undivided attention can improve your relational abilities and fortify your associations with others.

Chapter 3:

Unlocking the Secrets of Effective Selling Strategies

Are you having trouble achieving your sales objectives? Are you looking for a secret that will convert potential customers into devoted clients? Look no further because I'm going to tell you the three selling secrets that helped me build two successful businesses that have each made millions of dollars in revenue. The most outstanding aspect? You can improve your sales game right now by implementing these straightforward strategies.

1

Offering some incentive Forthright

In our current reality, where rivalry is furious and client assumptions are taking off, it's significant to stick out. One of my time-tested strategies includes offering some incentive upfront, long before the idea of procurement even enters the discussion. Initially, this strategy may seem counterintuitive, but it has repeatedly proven to be revolutionary.

Throughout the course of recent years, I've committed myself to creating educational recordings, adroit posts, articles like this one, and useful meetings on digital broadcasts. Not only do these actions demonstrate my expertise, but they also offer insights that can be put into action and address real issues. My trip to Spain, where I had the honor of giving a speech at the prestigious University of Pompeu Fabra, is one memorable memory. This opportunity demonstrated the impact of free knowledge sharing.

All the more so as of late, my group and I fostered a significant device that cost us about $10,000. We decided to give it away for free rather than make money off of its value. This tool, which shows how much it will cost to decommission solar systems, was more than just a number; it also showed our commitment to giving our audience more power. By embracing the way of thinking of giving prior to getting, we lay out trust and compatibility that can't be accomplished through simple deal strategies.

2

Building legitimate connections

Building certified associations has turned into an uncommon item during a time when mechanized messages and generic corporations have become the standard. However, it's precisely this personal touch that can set you apart in the sales world. As opposed to plunging heedlessly into an attempt to sell something, I focus on laying out an earnest association with likely clients. Simply ask my companion Michael Birchall about the 20-minute irregular discussion we had today on the crazy advantages of plant-based slimming and the old-matured intelligence of granddads we never met, followed by a speedy 2-minute discussion about a potential half-million dollar bargain.

Think about it: when was the last time a sales pitch that felt more like a conversation actually engaged you? We create an atmosphere where people are more receptive to hearing about our products or services by concentrating on the development of bonds and common ground. These interactions are built on laughter and meaningful connections, allowing for a smooth transition into the sales discussion.

3

Making a big difference Despite the fact that the word "sales" often conjures up images of closing deals and earning commissions, there is a more important aspect that is often overlooked. This is the most important lesson I've learned: A commission may be paid for transactions based on price, but a lifetime fortune may be earned for transactions based on genuine assistance.

Stepping in to help somebody in need isn't just about the monetary rewards; it's also about the fulfillment of changing lives. Our reputation grows, and clients see us as more than just vendors; they see us as trusted partners and friends when we become positive change agents. This viewpoint shift improves our profound prosperity and raises our monetary outcome over the long haul.

In conclusion,secret formulas and intricate strategies do not guarantee success in sales. It's about adhering to simple but profound principles that align with our longing for genuine connection and benefit both parties. My sales philosophy is based on providing value right away, cultivating genuine relationships, and prioritizing meaningful impact. By involving these mysteries in your methodology, you'll reinforce your income and develop a tradition of trust and regard that stretches a long way beyond the domain of business. Keep in mind that people are more likely to do business with people they consider to be friends. Are you looking for sales strategies and advice to boost your business? It takes both hard work and the right skills to be a successful salesperson, but you can improve your performance with the right tools.

We are of the opinion that any competent salesperson—or any person at all—will always have room for development and skill enhancement in their position. As a result, we put a lot of money into our team's ongoing education, encourage them to read industry publications outside of work, and give them the opportunity to test their ideas with confidence that they will use the information to improve their work.

We have decided to share some of our advice with you because our salespeople have gained a lot of experience. The following is a list of our top twenty methods for selling that will help you become more successful.

You can't be an effective salesperson if you don't know who you're selling to and what the market landscape is like. This is the most important thing. We're not discussing simply knowing their name, title, organization name, site, and email. We're trying to figure out exactly what makes them tick.

What is a typical day like for your prospect? What difficulties do they face? What could simplify their lives?

You will be able to better understand how they can benefit from your solution and position your product or service in a way that will resonate with them if you acquire this information about your prospect.

You need to know not only what your prospects' problems are but also who else is trying to solve them for them outside of your business. How does the landscape of competition look? How does your answer compare? Do something different after examining the selling and pitching strategies of the competition.

You want to stand out and be different, but you still want to talk to people. Are you looking for sales strategies and advice that can help your business grow? It takes both hard work and the right skills to be a successful salesperson, but you can improve your performance with the right tools.

We are of the opinion that any competent salesperson—or any person at all—will always have room for development and skill enhancement in their position. As a result, we put a lot of money into our team's ongoing education, encourage them to read industry publications outside of work, and give them the opportunity to test their ideas with confidence that they will use the information to improve their work.

We have decided to share some of our advice with you because our salespeople have gained a lot of experience. The following is a list of our top twenty methods for selling that will help you become more successful.

You can't be an effective salesperson if you don't know who you're selling to and what the market landscape is like.

This is the most important thing. We're not discussing simply knowing their name, title, organization name, site, and email. We're trying to figure out exactly what makes them tick.

What is a typical day like for your prospect? What difficulties do they face? What could simplify their lives?

You will be able to better understand how they can benefit from your solution and position your product or service in a way that will resonate with them if you acquire this information about your prospect.

You need to know not only what your prospects' problems are but also who else is trying to solve them for them outside of your business. How does the landscape of competition look? How does your answer compare? Do something different after examining the selling and pitching strategies of the competition.

You need to stick out and be one of a kind while still addressing what your possibilities need.

In this video, our principal growth advisor discusses the significance of comprehending your target audience and some additional sales strategies that she has acquired while working at New Breed.

2. Center around the right leads.

As indicated by Ken Krogue, organizer and board member from InsideSales.com, "it's truly about the leads. From our perspective, this means knowing what makes a lead a good fit for your business so that you don't waste time on people who won't buy from you.

The first step in this sales strategy is to identify your target audience by creating buyer personas and ideal customer profiles. You should be able to figure out what they're having trouble with, what obstacles they face, and how your offers and messaging can be tailored to address their issues.

Better win rates, larger average deal sizes, and higher customer lifetime value are all results of focusing on the right leads. It's easier to keep them as customers if you focus on the people who will benefit most from your solution.

You'll be able to close more deals and save time by not having to spend as much time selling to them. You simply need to guarantee that your timing is correct and that they're prepared for what you're advertising.

Identify your most promising leads by utilizing data and analytics.

It is essential to have reliable data and analytics in order to effectively target the appropriate leads. You can identify patterns and characteristics that indicate which leads are more likely to become customers by analyzing your previous sales and marketing efforts. Lead scoring and predictive analytics can be utilized to prioritize leads according to their likelihood of conversion. You will be able to concentrate your efforts and time on the leads that have the greatest potential to sell.

3. **New Breed emphasizes that selling is a collaborative activity.**

Put your business first. The advertising group assists the deals with joining. Members of the sales team support one another. The same end goal is achieved by each team member and individual: assisting the company's expansion.

Every time you make a decision, keep in mind that same philosophy. Customers should come first, followed by your business, team, and yourself.

4. **Influence Your**

At New Variety, we honestly love Salesforce. It serves as the CRM platform for our sales team, but we have also integrated it with HubSpot, our marketing automation software, to ensure complete communication between sales and marketing. Our sales team can see how a prospect has interacted with our content or their digital body language.

We can get a better sense of what they are interested in, what their pain points are, and how they came to know about us in the first place by knowing what blog posts they've read, pages they've visited, and emails they've opened.

If we notice that a person is reading content about conversion strategies, we can examine how they are converting visitors to customers on their website and provide tailored feedback during our initial outreach that demonstrates our comprehension of their challenges and how we can address them.

5 Be informed.

At the point when you're a little organization like us (really, this sounds valid regardless of whether you're a huge organization), efficiencies can help enormously. To determine what is effective and what is not, pay close attention to your metrics and marketing funnel. What is assisting your sales team in making more sales? What do they appear to be stumbling over?

Listening to the numbers is a crucial part of your sales success because data doesn't lie.

We realize that information examination can require some investment, so in the event that you're not acclimated with estimating your deal endeavors, begin with semiannual reports and make them as top-to-bottom and nitty-gritty as could be expected. When you reach that point, begin submitting quarterly reports. These can be somewhat lighter than the semiannual ones, but they ought to, in any case, contain nitty-gritty measurements. Then, at that point, go as granular as month to month. This can be the lightest of the three renditions, and it simply checks out your deals on a more elevated level.

Each report should try to show you something from a different point of view. You can make better decisions and get better results in the long run by looking at different trends.

6. **Truly pay attention to your prospects.**

This business procedure eventually comes down to trust. As per Imprint Roberge, the previous head of HubSpot's Business Division, "You realize you are running a cutting-edge outreach group while selling feels more like the connection between a specialist and a patient and less like a connection between a sales rep and a possibility."

Anyway, what's the significance of that?

We must be able to listen to our customers in order to be successful salespeople. We will quite often be an egotistical culture, to a limited extent on account of virtual entertainment, so it's vital that, as a sales rep, you care about your possibilities—and not simply on a superficial level. That will radiate through in your discussions, assist with building trust, and assist with closing bargains.

7. Establish credibility through education.

When attempting to sell a product or service, establishing credibility can be challenging. We've been molded to have a terrible response to a "sales rep," as they've been described as vile and conniving.

So today, you must encourage that relationship and entrust it with your possibilities. Education is a great way to achieve this.

At the point when we say instruction, we're truly discussing your substance. Your blog, premium content offers, webinars, and other content can all be used to educate your prospects about your company's offerings.

Do not immediately go for the hard pitch. In the event that you help to teach them, empowering them to go with their own choices (which you've helped guide toward your answer), they will start to trust you. Additionally, gaining trust increases your chances of winning the relationship.

To benefit the most from your instructive efforts, customize your endeavors. Sending a similar blog entry to 20 individuals is simply showcasing deals in a one-on-one discussion.

Rather than sending along a blog entry or online course without anyone else, take a statement from a significant substance offering and apply it explicitly to your possibility to give instruction and influence the substance you have yet to be human.

8. Focus on helping

How frequently do you receive a call from a salesperson in which they solely discuss the brand-new features of the product they are selling? You listen amenably, yet contemplate internally, "Definitely, yet how does this help me?"

The reality is that features are useless to you. In the manner they're normally situated by deals. is what you really want to know. You basically want to know how the offer will solve your problems.

This differentiation is essential for salespeople. Consider how your solution's features can benefit your prospect rather than its features. How are you dealing with one of their problems or difficulties?

If you know who your buyer personas are, you will know what problems they face and how your solution addresses those issues. This is your chance to emphasize the advantages of your product or service or how you can simplify that person's day.

At the point when you can hype up the advantages, you'll have a lot simpler time persuading possibilities that your association can most successfully settle their necessities.

9. End each gathering with an action.

At the point when you leave your next gathering, as opposed to expressing something like, "I'll circle back to you on our following stages," make your subsequent stages at that moment.

We tried this technique on our own outreach group and saw enormous outcomes. We used to say goodbye to a prospect at the end of our meetings by saying that they could anticipate hearing from us in a few hours at a few convenient times for our next meeting. It became increasingly difficult for us to schedule that subsequent meeting.

As a result, we decided to alter our approach. Presently, while we're finishing a deal call, we're finishing substantial activity. We, as a whole, draw up our schedules and book our next gathering on the spot. Furthermore, learn to expect the unexpected. We've seen our transformation rates increase because of it.

Avoid leaving a sales meeting with a empty stomach the next time. While you're there, set up your next meeting with the prospect, or at the very least come up with a specific plan of action that both parties can agree on.

10. **Make use of your marketing team.**

Your sales and marketing teams must be in sync. There's so much that these two divisions can learn from one another to assist the association in arriving at its fundamental objective of creating more income.

Make use of your marketing team to your advantage in sales. Ask them about the feedback from your customers—do they respond positively to a piece of content? Did they not partake in the online class they joined? Your marketing team can continue to supply you with increasingly high-quality leads if you share these insights with

Full straightforwardness will help you both be more successful.Your reports should also be shared with the marketing team. Promoting ought to empower your outreach group to find lasting success. A piece of that is conveying drives; some portion of that is empowering deals with great substance; and some portion of that is guaranteeing a smooth handoff. To accomplish all of those things, however, marketing must collaborate with sales.

At New Variety, we have an income group rather than isolated promoting and outreach groups, so showcasing and deals are adjusted behind a similar objective: bringing in money. Marketing is more motivated to attract high-quality leads with a high likelihood of becoming customers because their contribution to revenue is measured rather than the number of leads they generate.

Marketing, on the other hand, won't have access to the data they need to guarantee that they are providing sales with qualified leads if there isn't open communication between the two teams.

Getting customers takes time, but using sales strategies like prospecting and guiding those prospects to a secured sale can speed up the process.

Chapter 4

Strategies to find clients for business success

Conviction is 90% of a sale, and persuasion is 10%, says Indian author Shiv Khera, who has written a number of self-help and sales books in his career.

Obviously, most clients won't buy from you right away, so you want to foster a compelling arrangement to assist you in remaining in steady contact until they make a purchase from you.

Since customers are the foundation of every business, the various strategies and methods we will discuss in this article will focus on capturing them.

We trust that you will find them extremely valuable, so you can rapidly expand your client base.

Strategies for attracting clients effectively.

Study and grasp your ideal interest group.It might seem hard to miss, yet most organizations will more often than not naturally suspect they know who their clients are and who they don't.

Be that as it may, you really want to break it down over and over and make a nitty-gritty investigation of who the possible clients for your item or administration truly are.

This is a key stage, as it will give you the knowledge you need to contact these individuals and, most importantly, comprehend what their fundamental necessities are and how your business might have the option to meet them.

More sales and marketing strategies for attracting customers are available to you the more you learn about them.

Partner with businesses that complement your type of business.

It is very important to collaborate with businesses that can complement your business model to ensure a large number of future customers' participation.

For instance, in the event that you sell a line of shoes, you can cooperate with dress-centered organizations, where both of you could set up systems to get clients: notice in informal organizations or on the site, make retail locations with the two brands, promote on Google, and so on.

To put it plainly, it's a powerful method for catching traffic for your business, and in a manner, it assists the two organizations with creating a gain.

Participating in events is yet another strategy for attracting clients.

In recent years, this kind of strategy has gained a lot of popularity.

An ever-increasing number of individuals are sorting out occasions where they present new drives and are like gatherings," fully intent on uniting similar organizations and sharing encounters.

It additionally assists with drawing in clients from similar organizations and, accordingly, producing more deals in general.

For private companies, this methodology may not see any profit from speculation right away, but in the long run, it could have extraordinary advantages.

However, it appears that new strategies for attracting customers are being developed on a daily basis.

That is the reason we share with you these

reliable methods that can assist you with getting steadfast clients

for your business.

10 strategies on the best way to get new customers

These techniques have a demonstrated history of assisting organizations with creating top-caliber, high-change leads that practically move along automatically.

Among the methods we suggest are:

1) **Make a rundown to assist you with building your image on the Web.**

These days, being available online has turned into a vital activity to get clients.

Let's return to the shoe shop as an example: How do you expect your target audience to find you or be aware that you exist?

Nowadays, the majority of people search for nearby shoe stores on Google.

That is why you want to have an internet-based presence so your potential clients can undoubtedly find and purchase from you.

2) **Clarify some pressing issues and listen actively.**

At the point when you generally converse with your possibilities, it is fundamental that you pose applicable inquiries and listen effectively.

This will give you a better idea of how your potential customers see things, and listening will make your customers feel at ease and trust you.

3) **Joining groups that are related to your business is another way to get customers.**

"Being a part of communities that focus on your product or service in a similar way will help you feel like you belong to a group of people who have the same goals but take different approaches."

You'll learn more and get new ideas to use in your business from this.

You can find these groups online, but for better interaction, it's best to meet them in person.

4) **Get the most out of your social networks.**

Social media is a huge platform where a lot of potential customers look.

Social networks can help you boost sales and build your brand's reputation if used correctly and strategically.

a variety of tactics, including creating Facebook or Instagram ads or publishing quality content. This can help boost your website's traffic?

5) **Use email marketing.**

One of the best ways to generate leads without spending money on advertising is to use email marketing.

Ask your prospect for his email address when he visits your website. Additionally, this makes it simple to generate leads.

6) **Establish lasting relationships.**

When you run a small business, it becomes essential to establish lasting relationships with both your clients and employees.

When you have a good relationship with your coworkers, it's easy to work together and coordinate.

Your clients will also recommend you to their friends and family if you have a good relationship with them.

Remember: A customer who is recommended is covered!

7) When you get customers, show them how valuable you are. In every way you can, tell them about every good thing you've done for them and how you specifically helped them.

Your prospects will trust you more and be more likely to buy from you if you demonstrate your company's worth and capabilities.

8) **Go past after selling.**

It is fundamental that you go further, assuming you believe your clients should purchase from you over and over.

It is confirmed: Assuming your clients are cheerful, your business will keep on developing.

Be consistent with your services, regardless of whether your client is new or returning.

Your sales cycle will never end if you succeed.

9) **The individual effectively addresses all objections with a high level of professionalism.**

One of the most challenging aspects of the sales process is overcoming objections.

On the off chance that your possibility is posing a great deal of inquiries, this implies he is basically showing some interest.

Don't stop them from buying your product if they think it's too expensive; instead, keep convincing them why your product is important to them and how you can help.

However, if they believe that your company is not meeting their needs, try to consider their perspective before responding.

In like manner, attempt to defeat each complaint and don't surrender.

10) **It stands out from your rivals.**

In today's world, competition is fierce.

The same product or service will be offered by hundreds or even thousands of businesses.

As a result, you need to be extremely persistent in order to stand out.

However, do you know how to accomplish this?

Simple: when you're trying to get customers, point out any weaknesses you hear and show how your company is different from others in your industry.

Get customers right away!

Even if you don't use any of these strategies or techniques, getting new customers might seem like a difficult task at first. However, if you take the right steps, you can even travel across the seven seas.

Final summary

Delightful Sales Success" is a catchy title that conveys the accomplishment and contentment that come from a successful sales process. This synopsis will investigate how a mix of powerful deal strategies, consumer loyalty, and a charming encounter for the two clients and deal experts can prompt a magnificent deal achievement.

To make deals progress, organizations need to utilize different systems and strategies that resonate with their ideal interest group. This entails determining the requirements and preferences of customers, crafting persuasive sales pitches, and successfully negotiating deals. Notwithstanding, genuine progress goes beyond just making a deal.

Making the customer the most important thing is the foundation of delightful sales success. Businesses can create a positive customer experience by concentrating on providing exceptional customer service and cultivating relationships. Customers need to be heard, their concerns addressed, and solutions tailored to their specific requirements. At the point when clients feel esteemed and heard, they are bound to become recurrent clients and recommend the business to other people.

In addition, delightful sales success entails making sure that the sales procedure is enjoyable for